England
Is Truly A Magical Place

England
Is Truly A Magical Place

K M G Woodbury

ATHENA PRESS
LONDON

England Is Truly A Magical Place
Copyright © K M G Woodbury 2008

All Rights Reserved

No part of this book may be reproduced in any form
by photocopying or by any electronic or mechanical means,
including information storage or retrieval systems,
without permission in writing from both the copyright
owner and the publisher of this book.

ISBN 10-digit: 1 84748 191 4
ISBN 13-digit: 978 1 84748 191 7

First Published 2008
ATHENA PRESS
Queen's House, 2 Holly Road
Twickenham TW1 4EG
United Kingdom

Printed for Athena Press

For Kate and Sophia

Here is a tale of a girl and a chap
Travelling around England, so go get a map!
Follow their flight path, the places they linger;
Find each location with your finger!

All the things you will learn about,
There's more – so take some library books out!
Whatever you want to know, you can bet
You'll find it on the Internet.
But while it's a good and valuable mission,
Remember: ask Mum or Dad for permission!

The World is Truly a Magical Place

Jenny and Lenny, the mischievous twins
With muddied knees and gap-toothed grins
And rumbling tummies – they lick their lips;
It's time for fish fingers, beans and chips.
The clinking of plates and pots and pans,
Then Mum pipes up, 'Have you washed your hands?
Use soap and warm water, don't trick me,
Dirty digits and you'll get no tea!'
So Jenny and Lenny do as they're told;
On fish fingers night, they're good as gold.

A sound at the door, a key in the lock;
Dad must be home, it's seven o'clock.
The cuddling three go for their supper,
'You all right, Arthur? Fancy a cuppa?
How was your day, dear?' Mummy asks,
'Boring!' said Daddy, 'Menial tasks!'
He gently kisses his wife on the cheek;
A warm welcome home every night of the week.

'Mummy?' said Len, 'Do you know by chance,
What is the capital city of France?
We learned about it in geography today,
It's Paris or 'Pa-ree' as the French would say!'
A smiling daddy with his boy and girl,
'I wonder how much they know about the world?'

Their father, a kind and knowledgeable man;
As the kids gobbled up, so he began.
'The world is truly a magical place –
The plants, the animals and the human race.
The rivers and oceans, hills and mountains,
Cities and towns with squares and fountains.
Statues and monuments and all types of buildings
Standing majestic with their fine gold gildings.
Gardens with flowers and parks with trees,
The world, what a place! Ahhhh, the magic it weaves.'

'Come on you two, let's go over there;
Let's sit by the fire in our comfy chairs.'
First, Dad gave his specs a wipe;
Then with tobacco he filled his pipe.
'We haven't got long,' Daddy said,
'Just five minutes and it's off to bed.
Lenny at dinner you mentioned France,
We'll go in the summer if we get the chance.
Wherever you are, you'll be in a good mood,
Many people say France has the best food.
Down into Spain, a culture so full;
Where a man called a matador fights with a bull.
There's Austria and Switzerland with mountains of snow,
When skiing and sledging you shout, "Geronimo!"
In Japan you can ride the bullet train if you wish.
Or watch sumo wrestling while eating raw fish!
In Australia, "G'day" means "how do you do?"
And there's nothing quite like a kangaroo!

Africa is home to so many animals,
Birds and fish and reptiles and mammals.
America is where they make lots of movies,
Film stars and pop stars, who think they're so groovy!'

Jenny and Lenny thought the world sounds so cool
But tomorrow's approaching, another day at school.
Dad kissed them good night and off they went,
Straight up the stairs, they made their ascent.
Their mother was waiting, 'Now don't give me grief,
You must have a bath and then brush your teeth.
Then into bed and not a peep,
Turn out the light and go off to sleep.'

With jim-jams on, they got under the covers.
They whispered in a language unknown to all others.
Giggling and snorting, they're away with the fairies,
Away in twin-land, for how long? It varies!
Then Mum came in, 'Night-night my darlings,
Sweet dreams of robins and sparrows and starlings.'

Those sweet words echoed around in their ears;
They fell asleep together, so happy, no tears.
Flickering eyelids, they're having a dream;
The same dream, they are an inseparable team.
Of robins and starlings, like birds they were flying;
Through fluffy white clouds they were hardly trying.
Effortless gliding, they just looked so neat
With the breeze gently blowing on the soles of their feet.

A glorious blue sea with ripples of white,
As clear as day although it was night.
And back overland their flight is not over,
A sight to behold, the White Cliffs of Dover.
The same dream taking them back to twin-land?
Or an adventure in their home country… England!

SCOTLAND
Berwick-upon-Tweed
NORTH-UMBERLAND
Newcastle-upon-Tyne
Sunderland
Carlisle
Durham
DURHAM
Middlesbrough
CUMBRIA
Scarborough
Kendal
NORTH YORKSHIRE
Harrogate
York
EAST RIDING OF YORKSHIRE
Leeds
WEST YORKSHIRE
LANCASHIRE
SOUTH YORKSHIRE
Grimsby
Manchester
Liverpool
Sheffield
LINCOLNSHIRE
Chester
DERBYSHIRE
Lincoln
CHESHIRE
NOTTING-HAMSHIRE
Stoke-on-Trent
Derby
Nottingham
Grantham
King's Lynn
Norwich
Shrewsbury
STAFFORD-SHIRE
Leicester
Oakham
RUTLAND
NORFOLK
LEICESTER-SHIRE
Corby
Peterborough
WALES
SHROPSHIRE
Birmingham
WARWICK-SHIRE
NORTHAMPTON-SHIRE
CAMBRIDGE-SHIRE
Bury St Edmunds
Coventry
Bedford
Worcester
Northampton
Cambridge
SUFFOLK
Ipswich
HEREFORD-SHIRE
WORCESTER-SHIRE
BEDFORD-SHIRE
Hereford
BUCKINGHAM-SHIRE
HERTFORD-SHIRE
Colchester
ESSEX
Gloucester
Oxford
St Albans
GLOUCESTER-SHIRE
Beaconsfield
Southend-on-Sea
Swindon
OXFORDSHIRE
Windsor
GREATER LONDON
Bristol
WILTSHIRE
BERKSHIRE
AVON
Canterbury
Bath
Guildford
SURREY
KENT
Dover
SOMERSET
Salisbury
HAMPSHIRE
Taunton
WEST SUSSEX
EAST SUSSEX
Hastings
DEVON
DORSET
Southampton
Chichester
Brighton
Exeter
Poole
Weymouth
ISLE OF WIGHT
CORNWALL
Plymouth
St Austell
Land's End
SCILLY ISLES

The Garden of England

Beneath the twins, the county of Kent,
Green fields and orchards – heaven sent!
Apples, pears, plums and cherries;
Vegetable patches and forests of berries.
Centuries-old houses with fields of crops,
Special oast houses that dry the beer's hops!

A coastline dotted with castles and forts,
Dover's the busiest of all the world's ports.
A new way to Europe has now been paved;
The Channel Tunnel beneath these waves.

A man in a uniform holding a parcel,
The twins swoop down to Dover Castle.
'Good morning youngsters,' smiles the old man,
'My name is Roger, shake my hand.
Let me tell you a thing or three,
Of Kent and the city of Canterbury.
For religion in England, a lofty perch,
The Archbishop there is head of the Church.'

'Henry VIII had six wives indeed.
They lived in Kent castles at Hever and Leeds.
Catherine of Aragon and Anne Boleyn,
The first he divorced, the next was done in!

As Anne was a Queen to lose her head.
The next poor wife to share Henry's bed,
Was Jane Seymour, wife number three.
But after she died it was Anne of Cleves.
So, that's four wives he had so far
But then came the Catherines: Howard and Parr.
Howard was another sent for the chop;
But after Parr, the weddings would stop!
There's a little ditty to help you remember
The fate of the wives of this Royal member:
Divorced, Beheaded, Died,
Divorced, Beheaded, Survived.'

'To a house called Chartwell in the county's west,
A Prime Minister, Sir Winston Churchill, the best!
With the threat of the Germans invading our beaches,
He mobilised the country with stirring speeches.
In World War II, under pressure he thrived,
He led us to victory – 1945.'

'This wonderful castle here played its part
In rescuing troops, it was the heart.
In the cliffs below the castle, you know,
Was the nerve centre for Operation Dynamo.
In World War II, they made it work;
To save many soldiers stuck at Dunkirk.
All types of boats were sent to France
To give these troops another chance.
Returning, successful, through waves and drifts,
Co-ordinated here inside these cliffs.

A telephone exchange and rooms for codes,
A hospital too with wounded – loads.
Dover Castle had its say
So many could fight another day!'

'The Isle of Sheppey, 1909,
England's first ever in a straight line:
I'm talking about a flight in a plane,
The pilot – John Brabazon – that was his name.
But listen, I spied with my little eye
That you little cuties have learned to fly!
There's plenty of life left in these old arms
So let's fly together to see England's charms.
Up the east coast, we'll head to the north;
We'll come down the west, the centre, go forth!'

'Lenny, there's so much in England to see.
Let's fly like the wind,' said Jenny with glee.
'Roger, oh thank you, let's fly together;
Show us all of England, no matter the weather!'
Lenny let out a massive roar,
The excitement inside him had come to the fore!

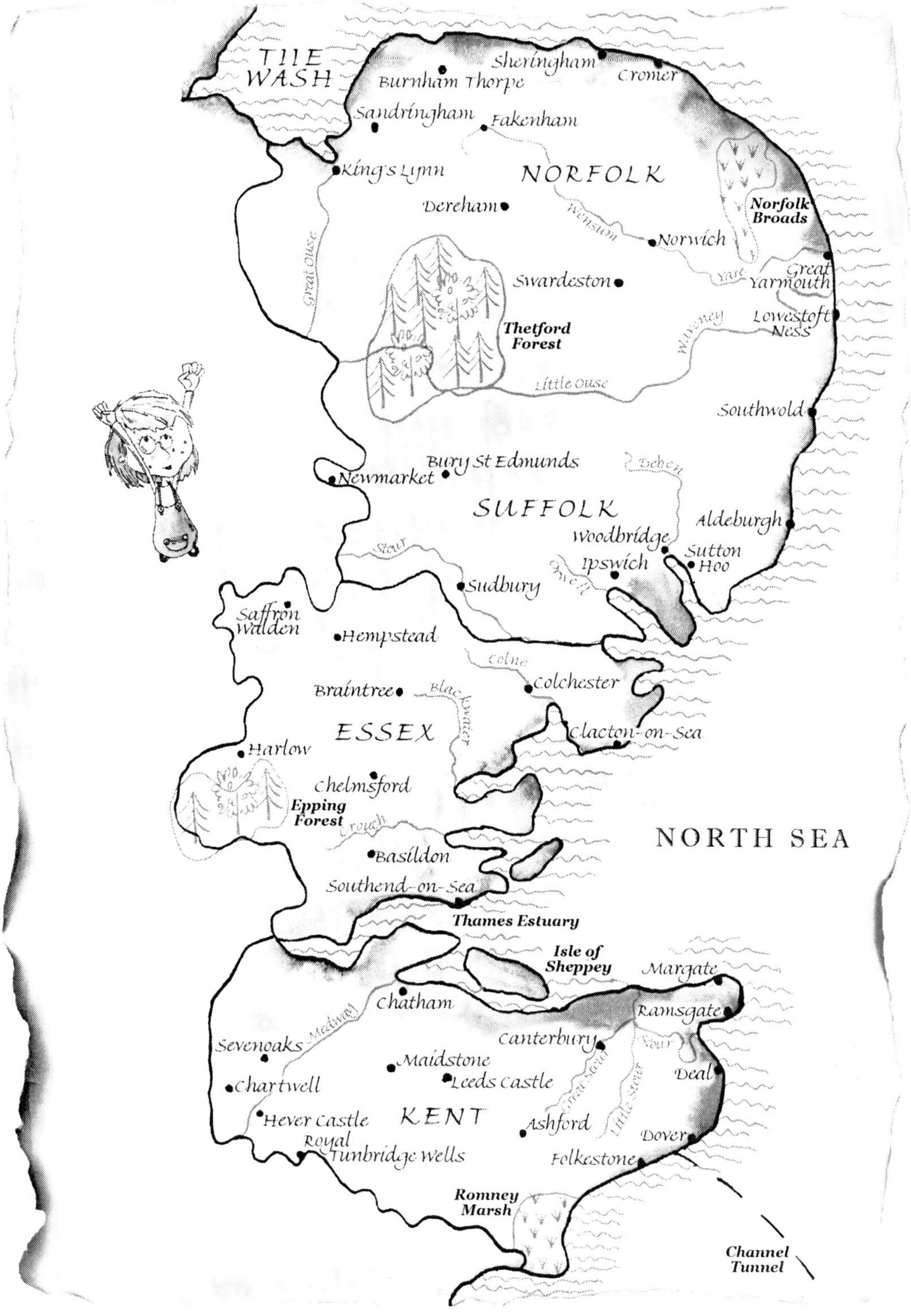

THE WASH
Sheringham
Cromer
Burnham Thorpe
Sandringham
Fakenham
King's Lynn
NORFOLK
Dereham
Norfolk Broads
Wensum
Norwich
Great Ouse
Swardeston
Yare
Great Yarmouth
Thetford Forest
Waveney
Lowestoft Ness
Little Ouse
Southwold
Bury St Edmunds
Deben
Newmarket
SUFFOLK
Aldeburgh
Woodbridge
Stour
Sutton Hoo
Ipswich
Orwell
Sudbury
Saffron Walden
Hempstead
Colne
Colchester
Braintree
Blackwater
ESSEX
Clacton-on-Sea
Harlow
Chelmsford
Epping Forest
Crouch
NORTH SEA
Basildon
Southend-on-Sea
Thames Estuary
Isle of Sheppey
Margate
Chatham
Ramsgate
Medway
Sevenoaks
Canterbury
Stour
Maidstone
Leeds Castle
Deal
Chartwell
Great Stour
Little Stour
Hever Castle
KENT
Ashford
Dover
Royal Tunbridge Wells
Folkestone
Romney Marsh
Channel Tunnel

A Star (or two) in the East

Over the water, Southend is near;
They're gliding over the world's longest pier.
Heading for Chelmsford and farmland views,
The home of the world's first radio news!
Colchester can wait, they fly north instead,
Roger shows them the village of Hempstead.
'Dick Turpin was born here, 1706,
A highway robber with plenty of tricks.
He paid for crimes he did on his horse –
The hangman's noose up at York racecourse!'
Now to Colchester, army garrison town;
The Romans' capital of some renown.

A perfect sky of cloudless blue;
Just east of Ipswich, the Sutton Hoo.
Buried in mudflats by the River Deben,
A Saxon long ship and a king long in heaven.
To Aldeburgh and Southwold, delightful resorts
With queues for chips and fish of all sorts.
Along the coast is Lowestoft Ness,
England's most easterly point no less.

Roger began, 'The last East Anglian king
Was Edmund, who endured such a terrible thing.
Against any battle over hill and ridge,
He wished for peace so hid under a bridge;

But the Viking hordes despised this bloke,
He was tortured and murdered and tied to an oak.
This was 870, maybe 869,
Bury St Edmunds, the abbey his shrine.'

The three soar above holiday hordes,
Enjoying the scenery, the Norfolk Broads.
The city of Norwich, the port of King's Lynn,
The River Ouse where The Wash comes in.
Roger told stories and led the way,
The twins hung on to every word he would say.
Norfolk and onward, through winds they'd prevail,
The white-bearded man recalled tale after tale…

'In World War I behind enemy lines,
A Norfolk nurse in Belgium shines.
Edith Cavell saved so many lives;
Helping the British escape to their wives.
The Germans found out – oh dear God!
They executed her by firing squad.
A heroine so brave, she gave her all,
She's buried now at Norwich Cathedral.'

'History records are all in awe
Of Nelson, "Britannia's God of War".
A naval captain, a Norfolk man,
A sharp tactician with a cunning plan.
When Napoleon wanted all Europe for the French,
Horatio Nelson kicked up a stench!

The French and Spanish had joined together
But he wanted England, English forever.
In 1805, he thought they were vulgar
So beat them in battle, in Spain at Trafalgar!
Today in London, a monument, not solemn,
A wonderful tribute called Nelson's Column.'

'In 1216, in the Fens swampy marsh
With whirlpools and mudflats and currents so harsh,
King John and his men crossed in bad weather.
Their horse-carts laden with gold and treasure.
Some soldiers and the Crown Jewels were lost,
The king hadn't long to count the cost.
He died by the time a week came around.
Today, these Crown Jewels are yet to be found!'

'Cambridge is famous for its university,
Made up of colleges like Jesus and Trinity.
As well as a city of scholarly faces,
Nearby the domain of Air Force bases.
Not just the British, the Americans too
Who flew side by side in World War II.'

'A Hertfordshire lady was hunted with venom,
Accused of being a witch was Jane Wenham!
Back in 1712 at court,
The evidence was heard, a verdict was sought.
But the judge wasn't sure why the jury had hardened
So he asked Queen Anne for a royal pardon.

So Jane went free and she had the last laugh
For the law was soon abolished on witchcraft!'

The twins delight in the thrills and spills,
They weave in and out of the Chiltern Hills.
In Beaconsfield, or on its edges,
Enid Blyton's house, 'Green Hedges'.
Another large house, but nothing sinister,
Is Chequers – the country home of the Prime Minister.

'In World War II, a risk and a chance,
Sending news – the resistance in France.
Woburn Abbey was message HQ,
'Watch out, the Germans are coming for you!'
German codes were cracked in a complex
At Bletchley Park, known as Station X!'

'At Tempsford nearby, stiff upper lip,
The RAF and their secret airstrip!
Nearby in RAF Twinwood's log,
The record of Glenn Miller's flight in the fog.
This famous bandleader and some of his men
Disappeared… and never were seen again.'

The twins were upset at this latest news,
On to Northampton where they make the best shoes!
And up the road is Althorp Estate,
Where Princess Diana is buried by a lake.
So tragic that she should die so young,
The 'people's princess' so full of fun.

'Across to Daventry where Sir Robert Watson-Watt
Discovered Radar which helped a lot!
The pilots were happy; the Air Force was smitten,
It helped to win the Battle of Britain!'

'Up to Naseby where in 1645,
King Charles I escaped with his life.
His Royalist Cavaliers were no more;
They lost the battle and the Civil War.
The Roundheads triumphant, all had gone well
For England's new leader, Oliver Cromwell.'

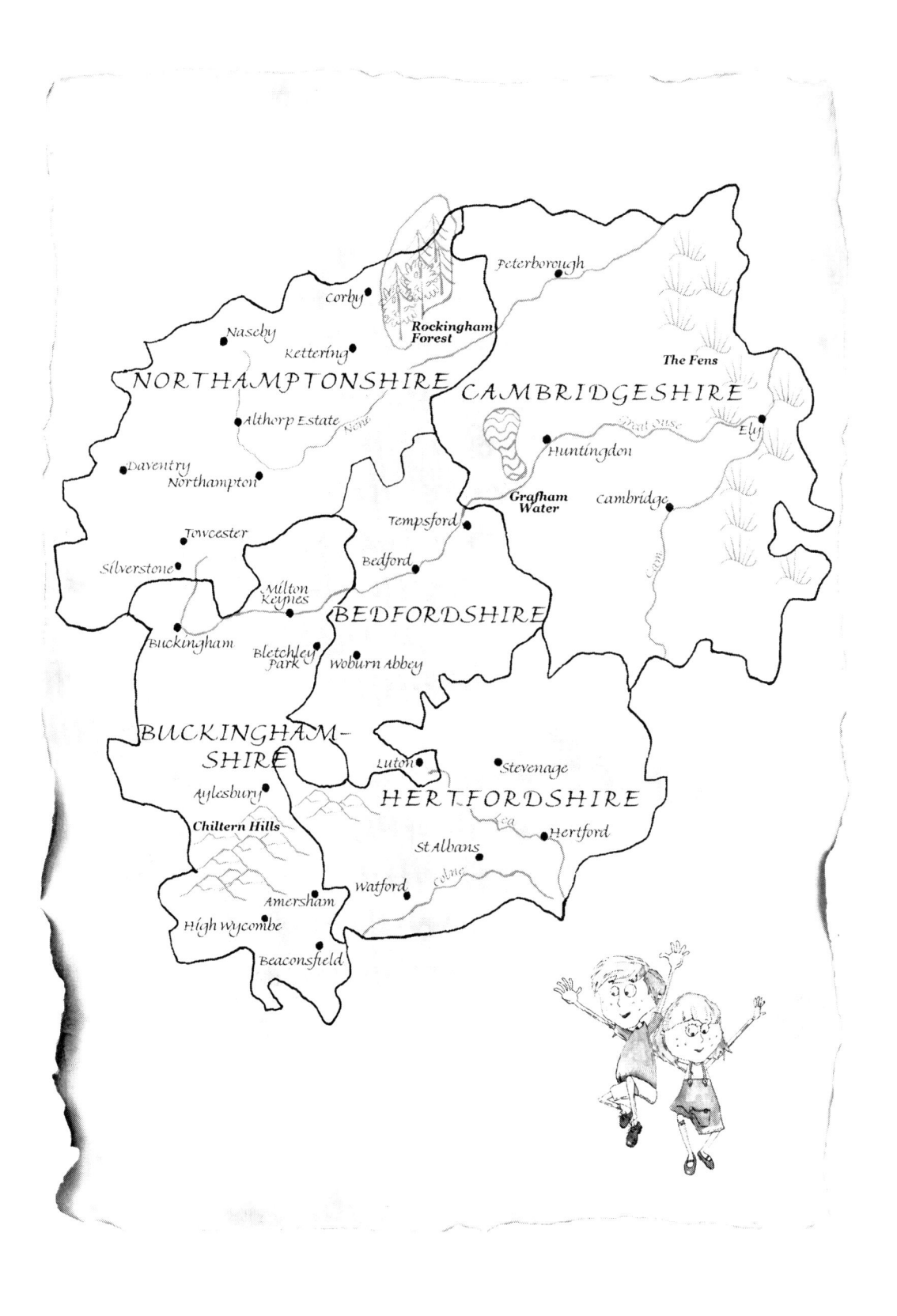

NORTHAMPTONSHIRE

- Naseby
- Corby
- Kettering
- **Rockingham Forest**
- Althorp Estate
- Daventry
- Northampton
- Towcester
- Silverstone

CAMBRIDGESHIRE

- Peterborough
- **The Fens**
- Huntingdon
- **Grafham Water**
- Cambridge
- Ely

BEDFORDSHIRE

- Tempsford
- Bedford
- Milton Keynes
- Bletchley Park
- Woburn Abbey

BUCKINGHAMSHIRE

- Buckingham
- Aylesbury
- **Chiltern Hills**
- Amersham
- High Wycombe
- Beaconsfield

HERTFORDSHIRE

- Luton
- Stevenage
- St Albans
- Hertford
- Watford

Let's Take a Peak

Across the border in Leicestershire,
The Wars of the Roses ended here.
The House of York's fate was sealed
When they lost the battle at Bosworth Field.
King Richard III lost his head
And many followers were also dead.
Henry VII after the war
Threw Richard's body in the River Soar.

The twins and Roger, at a pace much gentler,
Fly over Leicester and the National Space Centre.
On spotting, up ahead, the Peak District,
They flap their arms and stretch and kick.
Here was the 'Battle of Kinder Scout',
A battle with no armies or soldiers about!
But back in 1932,
A protest, a march, that now benefits you.
The Peak District, a place of beauty,
Was closed to the public with guards on duty!
Walkers from Manchester came from the west,
To trespass and protest with vigour and zest.
And hikers from Sheffield came from the east,
Determined and passionate, not scared in the least.
These ordinary people all used their feet
To come together in the centre and meet.

The police moved in and made some arrests
But a moral victory, the future attests.
These walkers here have left their mark
For soon it became a National Park.
Kinder Scout is the highest peak
Measuring just over 2,000 feet.

Through the wooded valleys they glide
Until they come to a permanent landslide!
'Shivering Mountain' called Mam Tor,
It shudders and slides across the floor!

On to Nottingham, the city of lace;
Close to the outskirts, a legendary place;
Where people were robbed time and again
By Robin Hood and his band of men.
In Sherwood Forest they had their own law:
'Steal from the rich and give to the poor!'

Over the cornfields, the wind was quite cool,
Then Jenny told them of a project from school.
'One day in 1662,
Young Isaac Newton was enjoying the view.
Under a Lincolnshire tree, it is said,
An apple fell upon his head.
Because of this, he wondered and frowned,
"Why does everything always fall… down?"
He studied hard, his main activity,
And later discovered the Theory of Gravity!'

'Also in Grantham, 1925,
A lady was born that ruled our lives.
Margaret Thatcher, to boos and cheers,
Was the Prime Minister for eleven years.'

Roger clapped and it was now Lenny's turn,
To share from school what he had learned.
'The Dambusters flew with aplomb
With Barnes Wallis' bouncing bomb.
From RAF Scampton to the dams on the Ruhr;
Their place in history is forever assured.
The Germans suffered, supply lines lost;
For Guy Gibson, a medal – the Victoria Cross!'

'The Lincolnshire coast, a long sandy strip
From Grimsby down to the southern tip,
Gibraltar Point, where birds like to flock
And cranes in summer perch on a rock.
Up the coast when it's high tide,
Grey seals sometimes enjoy the ride.
They come in to pup on the sand dunes
While starlings and thrushes whistle their tunes.'

Roger was delighted with this little bunch,
He decided to treat them to a fine English lunch.
'For Grimsby fishermen, danger lingers!
Remember this when you next have fish fingers.
To bring in a catch, to earn them some pay,
These fishermen risk their lives each day;

In very rough seas, by day and by night,
In walls of black waves with froths of white!
Let's eat and thank fishermen and praise be to God
For chips, crispy batter and white chunks of cod!'

NORTH SEA
Humber
Scunthorpe
Grimsby
High Peak
Lincoln Heath
Lincoln Wolds
Kinder Scout
Mam Tor
Worksop
Scampton
Lincoln Marsh
Peak District
Chesterfield
Lincoln
Buxton
Mansfield
Derwent
LINCOLNSHIRE
Skegness
Sherwood Forest
DERBY-SHIRE
Dove
Newark
Witham
Gibraltar Point
NOTTINGHAM-SHIRE
Ashbourne
Trent
Boston
THE WASH
Derby
Nottingham
Grantham
The Fens
Loughborough
Spalding
Oakham
Welland
LEICESTER-SHIRE
Melton Mowbray
Rutland Water
Stamford
Bosworth Field
Leicester
Soar
Hinckley
RUTLAND

Go Forth to the North

The flying trio, the cold they now feel
Approaching Sheffield, the city of steel.
So next time you sit down to eat roast pork
It may say 'Sheffield Steel' on your fork!
Yorkshire's a county of varied beauty,
A county of culture and unashamed nudity!
Where men stripped off in the film, *The Full Monty*.
There are also three authors, the sisters Brontë,
That's Anne, Charlotte and Emily,
Imagine that, such a talented family!

The other towns offer many treats,
Renowned as the home of certain sweets.
Halifax is known as 'Toffee Town'
While Pontefract is 'Liquorice Town'.
Many towns had the same goal
To earn a living mining for coal.

'Roger,' said Jenny, 'Tell us more,
You must have lots more tales in store!'

'Well here, in 1853,
A plane was built by Sir George Cayley.
A boat-shaped cockpit, a tricycle below,
With wings of cloth, he gave it a go.

He summoned his driver, John Appleby,
"Strap yourself in and that will be
The chance of a lifetime, mark my words,"
But poor John thought it quite absurd.
Still, off he was pulled down the hill,
Over a ledge… it's now God's will!
While thinking, "Why me? This is not fair."
The "plane" took off and flew through the air!
Soon, however, poor John found
His plane had crashed down into the ground.
Unhurt, he said, "I'm no flying gopher,
I'm leaving and I'm no longer your chauffeur!"
What he didn't know, after this fright;
He was the pilot of the world's first flight…'

'Religion has always had a major role to play
In England, through the centuries and still so today.
At one time people worshipped pagan gods
But old King Edwin was at odds.
The Great Council gathered near York;
At Londesborough, where they had a talk.
A decision was taken in 627
To become Christians and end up in heaven.'

'That is the word of religious historians.
Now, most people here are still Christians.
47.3 million is England's population
And many religions make up this great nation.

There are also Sikhs, Muslims and Jews,
Buddhists and Hindus with differing views.
People have come here from everywhere
With families to live, a new life to share.
However, we do have some racist fools,
Who shout rude things and bully in schools.
These are the cowards, who are a disgrace,
For different cultures should be embraced.
Most of us welcome the smiling faces;
England – a land of proud mixed races.'

'There are so many things to say
About people and places up this way.
Like William Bradley, a record he clinches,
The tallest man – seven feet nine inches!
Captain James Cook, he was no failure
For he was the one who discovered Australia!
And at the village, Wold Newton, no lie;
A meteor from space fell from the sky!
It just missed a man, within an inch of his life,
This was in 1795.
Today, you can see it just for some fun
At the Natural History Museum, London!'

The three were now over a medieval village!
They imagined a time of invasion and pillage.
Deserted now is Wharram Percy,
But well looked after, it's at your mercy!

Jenny took off at quite a pace,
So Lenny and Roger were quick to give chase.
Jenny pointed to the walled city of York
Then signalled to Roger to begin his talk.

'Nowhere in Europe's more haunted than York
Where Roman, Saxon and Viking ghosts talk!
A plumber was working at Treasurer's House;
He heard a noise, was it a mouse?
No, a voice that made a call,
Then a Roman soldier came out of the wall!
His cart-horse and other soldiers followed,
The terrified plumber's legs went hollow.
As fast as he could the plumber did flee,
That was 1953.'

Roger kept talking without a pause,
Now they were over the North York Moors.
'That Harry Potter has thrilled a nation,
And Goathland here was Hogsmeade station!
South of Scarborough is Flamborough Head,
The oldest lighthouse in England, it's said.
Along to Whitby and views spectacular,
Here was set some chapters of *Dracula*!'

Away in the clouds, there's patchy weather,
Below, the Moors and purple heather.
In spring, the woods are alive with smells
And a vibrant carpet of bluebells.

Invoice for DjmQVgnDR 25 April, 2008

amazon.co.uk

www.amazon.co.uk

Invoice/Receipt for

Your order of 25 April, 2008
Order ID: 203-5291218-7533956
Invoice number: DjmQVgnDR
Invoice Date/Date of Supply: 25 April, 2008

Paid by

Celia Sweetman
41 Creffield Road
London, W5 3RR
United Kingdom

London, W5 3RR
United Kingdom

Qty	Item	Our Price (excl. VAT)	VAT Rate
1	England Is Truly a Magical Place KMG Woodbury 1847481914 Paperback	£5.49	0.00%

Shipping SubTotal (excl. VAT)
Order Total
Sale order paid by Visa
Balance Due

Conversion rate £1.00 (EUR 1.26)

This shipment completes your order

You can always check the status of your orders or change your account details from the "Your Account" link at the top of each page on our site.

Thinking of returning an item?

PLEASE USE OUR ON-LINE RETURNS SUPPORT CENTRE

Our Returns Support Centre (www.amazon.co.uk/returns-support) will guide you through our Returns Policy printable personalised return label. Please have your order number ready, (you can find it next to your order). Our Returns Policy does not affect your statutory rights.

Amazon EU S.a.r.l. 5, Rue Plaetis L - 2338 Luxembourg
VAT number: GB727255821
Please note - this is not a returns address - for returns - please see above for details of our returns policy.

Thank you for shopping at Amazon.co.uk!

19/DjmQVgnDR/-1 of 1-//1PMN/premium-uk/3603860/0425-22-00/0425-18-08 Pack Type: ON/60

The steady flow of westerly winds
Assist old Roger and the travelling twins.
West of Harrogate, hills and vales;
They're fast approaching the Yorkshire Dales.
Grassy pastures and wooded hills, steep,
And shaggy black-faced, curly-horned sheep!
Fields divided by walls of stone,
An ideal place to be alone.
Sunshine, then rain and sometimes snow,
The skies are garnished with colourful rainbows.
Waterfalls, boulders and dark caves,
At Malham Cove, a great stone wave!
A 265-foot wall
That 'only' dates back to the Ice Age, that's all!

SCOTLAND
NORTH SEA
WALES
Berwick-upon-Tweed
Holy Island
Farne Islands
NORTH-UMBERLAND
Alnwick Castle
Rothbury Forest
Cheviot Hills
Coquet
Newcastle-upon-Tyne
Hadrian's Wall
Tyne
Sunderland
Carlisle
Eden
Nenthead
Durham
Wear
DURHAM
CUMBRIA
Lake District
High Force
Cauldron Snout
Tees
Darlington
Middlesbrough
Stockton-on-Tees
Whitehaven
Scafell Pike
Lake Windermere
Coniston Water
Kendal
Lune
Swale
Whitby
North York Moors
Goathland
PENNINES
NORTH YORKSHIRE
Scarborough
Thirsk
Ripon
Ure
Yorkshire Dales
Wharram Percy
Flamborough Head
Wold Newton
Bridlington
Skipton
Harrogate
Wharfe
York
Morecambe
Lancaster
EAST RIDING
Ouse
WEST YORKSHIRE
Londesborough
Blackpool
Ribble
Burnley
Bradford
Leeds
Kingston-upon-Hull
Humber
Preston
Blackburn
Halifax
Pontefract
LANCASHIRE
SOUTH YORKSHIRE
Manchester
Liverpool
Mersey
Sheffield

The Angels of the North

Into Teesdale, the three are on course
For England's biggest waterfall, High Force.
The River Tees flows from the top
Down seventy feet, that's quite a drop.
Then just a little further out,
Another waterfall, Cauldron Snout.
The longest in England at two hundred feet,
Unspoilt and beautiful, nature's treat.

Young Lenny is a huge fan of trains,
Another chance to show off his brains!
'George Stephenson in 1825,
An engineer who changed people's lives.
He built the world's first railway with ease
From Darlington up to Stockton-on-Tees.'
Jenny giggled while Roger just smiled,
He took up the story from this clever child.

'Durham was the North's most powerful city
With a Norman Cathedral and strong university.
William the Conqueror had to enrol
Prince Bishops here, to keep control.
He trusted them and relied on them lots,
To govern the land and keep out the Scots!'

The Angel of the North, so neat,
Standing tall at sixty-six feet.
The largest sculpture in England to see,
In copper and steel by Anthony Gormley.
The twins sit proudly, each on a wing,
Crowned the North's new queen and king!

Roger continued to teach all he knew,
Impressive facts known to only a few!
'A Newcastle man was Sir Joseph Swan
But many people don't know what he's done.
He also invented the light bulb, that's right,
So was it he or Edison, who gave us light?'

'One of the greatest structures of all
Was built by the Romans: Hadrian's Wall.
Six years to build, digging up earth
From Newcastle over to Solway Firth.
Fifteen feet high and seventy miles long
And a number of Roman legions strong.
Built in AD 122
To watch the border, a perfect view!'
At Vindolanda, middle of the wall,
A museum with records can tell you all.

Over the wall on the other side,
Is England's quietest countryside.
The Cheviot Hills with millions of trees,
Red squirrels and otters do as they please.

Out to the east, by all reports,
Alnwick Castle was used as Hogwarts!
Just off the coast, the Christian high land
Of Lindisfarne, the Holy Island.
From here, religion was spread nationwide.
But if you visit, beware of the tide!

Roger continued, 'Just south of here,
The Farne Islands and a tale of cheer.
Nearly two hundred years ago,
A brave young girl in her boat did row.
A ship crashed and would soon be sinking
But Grace Darling was very quick-thinking.
She rowed out hard and saved five men,
She brought them in and went out again!
With the last four men safe in her boat
She became a heroine, she got their vote.
When word got around of this brave caper,
Grace had her photo in the newspaper!'

They all rest at the border a while,
Then fly near Scotland down to Carlisle.
A fortress city at Hadrian's Wall,
Jenny and Lenny are having a ball!
The Eden Valley has such sharp lines,
Its eastern wall is the rocky Pennines.
Not far from Hangman Hill, it's said,
Is England's highest village, Nenthead.

Better scenery they could not have picked,
The stunning landscape – the Lake District.
Red stone cliffs, out on the coast,
To England's highest mountain – a boast.
At 3,210 feet high,
The majestic peak of Scafell Pike.
The largest body of water is near,
A long thin strip, Lake Windermere.

The peace and quiet and the freedom to roam
Encouraged writers to make it their home.
A lady who lived here, a story plotter,
She wrote Peter Rabbit – Beatrix Potter.
Coniston Water, a setting so handsome
For *Swallows and Amazons* by Arthur Ransome.

'While there were stories,' said Roger, 'so magic,
In 1967… one tragic.
Trying to beat the world record for speed,
A terrible crash, so tragic indeed.
Donald Campbell in his beloved *Bluebird*
Was instantly killed at speeds, absurd.'

Away from the lakes they make their way;
Enjoying a cruise over Morecambe Bay;
Where shifting sands near the beach
Can leave walkers stranded and out of reach!

Jenny sees flashing lights on full power,
Then soon before her is Blackpool Tower!
The North, South and Central Piers,
Children with chips and adults with beers.
The Golden Mile, amusement arcades,
Blackpool Sands and donkey escapades.
Fairgrounds and rides, the place is pumping,
The twins even see people bungee jumping!

A Tale of Two Cities

Past the towns of Burnley and Blackburn,
The cotton industry was Lancashire's backbone.
Manchester, England's third largest city
With hard-working people, honest and gritty.
The twins are circling high above
Listening to Roger, his stories they love!

'In 1909, a remarkable antic,
The first to fly across the Atlantic,
A Manchester man named John Alcock,
Did it with sixteen hours on the clock.
Along with his navigator, Arthur Brown
From Canada to Ireland and safely down.'

'Liverpool, a port by the Irish Sea,
Just tucked inside on the River Mersey.
Slaves from Western Africa came
With traders "selling" these people – the shame!
Workers came over from Ireland and China
Packed in tight on ocean liners.
Shipping was vital, with cotton imported,
Then made into clothes to be exported.
Cruise liners ready with flags unfurled,
Luxury trips to the exotic new world.
A city that's home to entertainers galore
Including The Beatles, "The Fab Four".'

'Lenny, your friend with the engineer's brain,
George Stephenson built the world's fastest train.
Well, at least it was in 1829,
Thirty miles per hour down the line!
He brought his *Rocket* and gave it a tester
Between the cities of Liverpool and Manchester.'

On the other side of the Mersey
Is Birkenhead, not far from Wallasey.
Roger's face went suddenly pale,
He began to tell a very sad tale.

'A chilling tale of bravery, true.
A ship was built here, 1852,
The Navy's HMS *Birkenhead*
Sunk, with over 400 dead.
From Portsmouth down to the African coast,
Packed with reinforcement troops, most.
It hit a rock in the dead of night;
For soldiers and sailors, a terrible plight.
There were also women and children on board;
Lifeboats readied, Captain Salmond implored:
"To the lifeboats – women and children first!"
The ship was sinking, he feared the worst.
"Every man for himself," he then cried,
But the soldiers were told to stand aside.
Lieutenant Colonel Seton in charge,
Knew the risks to the lifeboats were large.
If too many people clambered in,
Survival chances for children were slim!

So he, the Captain, and many men
Stayed with the ship, never seen again.
Their sacrifice had saved many lives,
All the women and children survived…'

With tears streaming from their eyes,
The three continue across the skies.
Chester, a city for a Roman legion
Who kept control of the north west region.
They all go to visit the massive zoo,
No need for tickets, they fly on through!
Families in the comfort and safety of cars
See animals roaming – no cages, no bars!
Another place they go to view
Is England's oldest sporting venue.
Since 1540, home of the horse,
Gamblers too, Chester racecourse!

Home of the potteries, Stoke is near.
At Burton-on-Trent, they brew the beer.
So Roger nips off for a quiet drink,
The twins decide to have a think.
'I know,' said Lenny, 'over that side,
We'll have lots of fun on those scary rides!'
Lenny chuckles while Jenny cowers,
The terrifying rides of Alton Towers!

Liverpool
Birkenhead
The Wirral
Warrington
Mersey
Runcorn
Cheshire Plain
Wilmslow
Northwich
Macclesfield
Chester
Dane
CHESHIRE
Peak District
Crewe
Leek
WALES
Weaver
Stoke-on-Trent
STAFFORDSHIRE
Whitchurch
Uttoxeter
Oswestry
SHROPSHIRE
Stafford
Burton-upon-Trent
Trent Valley
Boscobel House
Shrewsbury
Cannock Chase
Lichfield
Shifnal
Iron Bridge
Wenlock Edge
Tamworth
Wolverhampton
Walsall
Severn
WEST MIDLANDS
Clun Forest
Wyre Forest
Birmingham
Ludlow Castle

The Workshop of the World

Into Shropshire on the border with Wales
With scenic hills and red earth vales.
A land of orchards and dewy petals,
The birthplace of industry using metals.
To English history, a stunning inclusion:
The start of the Industrial Revolution!
The world's first iron bridge was built
And factories too with production full tilt.
New buildings, equipment and all sorts of tools;
A new way of life, a new set of rules!

Roger caught up with the flyaway twins,
He scratched his beard, then he begins.
'In Shrewsbury, born in 1809,
Charles Darwin, who strived to define
The origins of man, their form, their shape;
He worked out we're all descended from apes!'

'Ludlow Castle was a royal home
To princes destined for the throne.
When Edward IV had passed away,
Two young princes made their way
To London, but they disappeared.
Murdered in the Tower it's feared
By their uncle, that's the word,
So he'd become King Richard III.'

'Just years later, a similar fate,
Which led to the crowning of Henry VIII.
His older brother Prince Arthur had died
But this time, no crime was implied.'

'The English Channel does flow and ebb,
But a Shropshire man, Matthew Webb,
In 1875 became
The first man to swim from Dover to Calais.'

'The oldest Englishman by far
Was Shropshire's own, Thomas Parr.
He lived to 152.
Eat up your greens and you could too!'

'Charles I buried Tom in Westminster,
Coming for him was something more sinister
As Oliver Cromwell beat Charles I.
For Charles II, it couldn't be worse.
He lost his father and his throne,
His right to rule was overthrown.
So to 1651,
The Battle of Worcester had to be won.
But Charles lost and made his escape,
His claim to the throne was in worse shape!
Cromwell's men hunted him down,
They searched and overturned each town.
Outside Shifnal at Boscobel House,
Charles was hiding, quiet as a mouse.

He couldn't be found. Where could he be?
Safely up an old oak tree!
He later moved on and took his chance,
He jumped on a boat and escaped to France.'

And so they land in England's second city,
Birmingham, with canals so pretty.
A massive network that rings the land,
This city is known as the 'Venice of England'.
Industrial hotbed that prospered and swelled,
For many years, 'the workshop of the world'.

All kinds of foods, a wonderful perk;
Like chicken that's spiced with Jamaican Jerk.
Fragrant dishes with ingredients so fresh,
The tastes of India, Pakistan, Bangladesh.
Museums and galleries, the city is vast,
Our three explorers are having a blast!
They join the locals who make a mad dash
To shop at the Bull Ring and spend their cash!
Then to a place they'll love, they will,
The famous chocolate factory at Bournville!

The author, Tolkien, wrote many things,
The Hobbit and *The Lord of the Rings*.
Birmingham was his inspiration,
On here, he modelled many a location.

The Severn Wonders of the World

Roger continued, 'A thousand years ago
A lady helped keep taxes low.
Her husband wanted to make them high
But Lady Godiva let out a sigh,
"Coventry folk don't have much money
So please don't tax them too high, honey.
If you cut taxes, without a frown,
I'll ride my horse, naked through town!"
Her husband agreed and people made sure
They showed her respect by staying indoors.
However, there was one naughty lad
Who watched her ride and that was bad.
They poked his eyes out for what he'd done,
From then, he was known as Peeping Tom.'

To Warwick Castle on the River Avon,
For some a prison and others a haven.
With towers and turrets and beautiful things,
With dungeons, a prison for earls and kings!

Stratford-upon-Avon's not far from here,
The home of the bard, William Shakespeare.
Playwright and poet, the master of rhyme,
Considered the greatest writer of all time.
The Vale of Evesham, with climate to suit
For growing vegetables and all kinds of fruit.

A man at the heart of Worcester's story,
Composer of *Land Of Hope and Glory*,
Edward Elgar wrote England's songs;
A national treasure – Last Night of the Proms!
Worcester lies on the River Severn,
A little slice of English heaven.
The cathedral, the boats and the cricket ground,
Traditional pubs and restaurants abound.
However it is also famous of course,
As the home of the spicy Worcestershire Sauce!

Roger sighed, 'In the houses here were Catholic priests
Who, in the 17th century were treated like beasts.
If they preached, there was retribution,
They were imprisoned, then execution!
They hid in "priest holes" – secret rooms
Behind false walls and cupboards for brooms.'

The views of seven counties spill
In all directions from the Malvern Hills.
Nine miles long and one mile wide,
Beautiful trails to lengthen your stride.
Our airborne three are beginning to weaken,
They rest at British Camp, Herefordshire Beacon.
And the purest springs they've ever seen,
Malvern Water, a favourite of the Queen!

To Herefordshire and a landscape wider;
The home of apples and making cider.

Orchards, forests, meandering rivers;
Wonderful nature in glimpses and slivers.
To Gloucestershire and the Forest of Dean,
The most beautiful place they've ever been!

Over the Severn with gusto and cheer,
Outside Tetbury, Prince Charles lives here;
At Highgrove House, his country estate.
He'll succeed the Queen as Head of State!
The air is fresh and the hills stand proud,
The twins lead the way across to Stroud.
Here, we have Reverend Awdry to thank,
A local and author of 'Thomas the Tank…'

'A title,' said Roger, 'That no one would want
Has been bestowed upon Joseph Delmont.
He threw down a glove, he followed the rule
But became the last victim of a pistol duel!'

'Edward II was a rotter and rascal;
So thought his captors at Berkeley Castle.
They left no marks on his body, not one,
They'd shoved a red-hot poker up his bum!
A shocking end for a king to befall,
Edward is buried at Gloucester Cathedral.'

Jenny and Lenny just giggled away,
When Jenny was calm, she had something to say.
'There's one more thing about Gloucester, actually.
Here is Europe's biggest ice cream factory!'

Cheltenham was famous for its saltwater Spa,
Here Roger told Lenny and Jenny, the star!
'A Cheltenham man, so brave and astute;
The first man down in a parachute.
John Hampton went up in a balloon;
He jumped out and hoped he would land safely soon!
In fact, just thirteen minutes all told;
In 1831, how bold!'

The Cotswolds is home to villages and towns
In hills of beauty, the views astound!
'Lenny,' said Roger, 'You love sport.
Well let me tell you of a different sort.
Every four years, we can watch the Olympics.
In 1612, they had the Cotswolds Olimpicks!
Archery, wrestling and riding horses;
Jumping and running round all sorts of courses.
However, with prizes rich for the picking,
The medieval sport of brutal shin-kicking!
They'd beat their shins with planks of wood
To toughen them up and prepare them, good!
Then in the contest, to laughs and hoots,
They'd kick each other with iron-tipped boots!'

'In recent times, the Olympic Games;
Outstanding achievements by English names:
Two gold medals for Dame Kelly Holmes,
Rowing's James Cracknell and Andrew Holmes.
King of the track and also the field,
Two golds was Daley Thompson's yield.

The gold medal battles, friend and foe;
A gold for Steve Ovett, two for Seb Coe.
In shooting, two golds for Malcolm Cooper
And two for sailing, Ben Ainslie, super!
All the Olympians were proud and brave
But the best of all – Sir Steven Redgrave.
He finished with five gold medals for rowing,
Sir Matthew Pinsent with four, is still going!'

Map

WORCESTERSHIRE
- Kidderminster
- Redditch
- Worcester
- Pershore
- **Malvern Hills**
- **Vale of Evesham**
- Evesham

WARWICKSHIRE
- Nuneaton
- Coventry
- Rugby
- Warwick Castle
- Studley
- Stratford-upon-Avon
- Avon

HEREFORDSHIRE
- Kington
- Leominster
- Bromyard
- Hereford
- Ledbury
- Ross-on-Wye
- **Golden Valley**
- Lugg
- Arrow
- Wye

GLOUCESTERSHIRE
- Tewkesbury
- Cheltenham
- **Cotswolds**
- **Forest of Dean**
- Gloucester
- Stroud
- Cirencester
- Berkeley Castle
- Tetbury
- Severn

One of England's Gems – the Thames

They all head east to Oxford's fair city;
Since the 12th century, the first university.
Among the teachers that there have been
Are C S Lewis and J R R Tolkien.
Tolkien wrote stories of a world much barmier
While C S Lewis wrote *The Chronicles of Narnia*.

'William Morris started making cars
In Oxford,' said Roger, 'And among the stars:
The *Mini* and the *Morris Minor*,
English icons, there couldn't be finer.
The *Morris Minor* was first off the line,
The *Mini* followed in 1959.'

Flowing through is the River Thames,
One of England's finest gems.
From Cirencester to the North Sea,
The longest river it happens to be
At 215 miles long.
Some say the Severn but they'd be wrong!
It's five miles longer that's fair to tell
But it's also partly in Wales as well.

'Oakley Court, near Bray, in the distance,
The headquarters of the French Resistance
In World War II. Then it became
The setting for buildings in movie fame;

Dracula's Castle, *St Trinian's* School,
Also, the *Hammer House of Horror,* so cool!'

Eton is one of England's best schools.
A proud tradition, a stickler for rules!
Princes William and Harry went here;
A family home, Windsor Castle is near.
For over 900 years it's been
A home for many a king and queen.
An array of monarchs from history, varied,
In St George's Chapel are buried;
Like Charles I and Henry VIII,
There are ten kings and queens to date.
More recently, the Queen Mother,
The Queen's sister, Princess Margaret, another.
In 1992, a fire!
The Queen was saddened but through her desire
She gathered the finest ladies and men
And put the castle together again!

At Windsor Great Park is Legoland,
In 4,800 acres of land.
Across the way is Runnymede.
In history, a place for an important deed.
King John had to sign the Magna Carta –
The Latin term for the Great Charter.
In 1215, the Barons dared
To keep the king honest and fair,
So he didn't steal land from others;
A charter of landowners, sisters and brothers.

WALES
BRISTOL CHANNEL
Mouth of the Severn
AVON
Bristol
Bath
Avon
Weston-Super-Mare
SOMERSET
Cheddar Gorge
Wookey Hole
Glastonbury
Bridgwater
Parrett
Cadbury Castle
Yeovil
Taunton
Minehead
Exmoor
Quantock Hills
WILTSHIRE
Sevenhampton
Swindon
Chippenham
Box Hill
Devizes
Pewsey
Westbury
Salisbury Plain
Longleat
Stonehenge
Salisbury
Fovant
OXFORDSHIRE
Banbury
Chipping Norton
Charwell
Bicester
Witney
Oxford
Thames
Thame
Henley-on-Thames
BERKSHIRE
Newbury
Reading
Bray
Eton
Windsor Castle
Windsor Great Park

The Rest of the West

Though London is near, they set a new course
To Wiltshire, the county of the white horse.
On hillsides, the grass has been cut away
To shape a horse from the chalk underlay.
White horses on the hills they all see
Near places like Westbury, Devizes and Pewsey.

In Sevenhampton, near Swindon, was born
The late Ian Fleming, an author we mourn;
As he wrote the tales of which we're all fond,
The adventures of 007, James Bond.
Also the story of a car in flight,
Chitty Chitty Bang Bang, much to our delight!

Around 5,000 years ago,
It was decided the forests must go.
On Salisbury Plain, the land was cleared,
Years later, a circle of stones appeared.
Weighing four tons each – no scales!
These bluestones came across from Wales.
Or was it Ireland? Or were the stones local?
There are many theories and people are vocal.
This is Stonehenge, place of mystery,
The earliest site in England's history?

Nobody knows who built it really
But pilgrims flock here daily, yearly.

Before Christianity, the Pagans prayed
Around the circle of stones they laid.
They felt connected to the sun and moon
With nature's four seasons they felt in tune,
And elements; earth, air, fire and water.
Their love of every son and daughter.
Stonehenge, for Pagan worship, in the main;
A burial chamber on Salisbury Plain.

Some Morris dancing has Pagan roots;
To help Mother Nature so each plant shoots.
For healthy livestock and bumper crops,
They dance in circles with claps and hops
And celebrate the earth, the coming of light;
They embrace nature from morning to night.

In chalk hills, just like the white horses,
Regimental badges of the armed forces.
Near Fovant, a World War I army camp
Where soldiers carved badges to leave their stamp;
To remember their comrades who died in the war;
Their memory and regiment lives on, evermore…

West of the plain, a real treat,
The three visit Europe's first safari park, Longleat.
Since 1966, a home
For wild animals to graze and roam.
Jenny said, 'I do beg your pardon,
But I just love the butterfly garden.'

Lenny replied, 'There are many ways
To find your way out of the maze.'
Roger was chuffed they were having fun,
As they all left, his stories began.

'In World War II, ammunition supplies
Were hidden away from German eyes!
In a railway tunnel at Box Hill,
Not far from Bath, hidden, ideal.
A maze of tunnels with tracks for trains,
A nuclear bunker for the greatest brains,
The Royal Family, the Government,
And scientists working on secret experiments.'

'The city of Bath is so named
For the healing waters, the Romans claimed.
They built big baths with water, purest,
They soaked in the hot springs Aqua Sulis.
Each day, it pumped a million litres,
Rich in minerals, one of its features.
At 46.5 degrees,
The Romans' pains away would ease…'

'Bristol, a port with a fine reputation
For shipping excellence and organisation.
If something's "all shipshape and Bristol fashion",
It's been done well with detail and passion.'

'In Bristol, a man from yesteryear,
Probably England's finest engineer.

Isambard Kingdom Brunel designed
The Clifton Suspension Bridge, so fine.
His Albert Bridge stretched wide and far
In Plymouth across the River Tamar.
Always so busy, no time to slack!
He laid down miles of railway track
And bridges and tunnels along the way;
In 1833, his heyday.
Never an opportunity to skip,
He designed and built many a steam ship.
A very powerful man in his day,
Engineers still follow his methods today!'

Cheddar Gorge and the Wookey Hole caves;
Ice Age splendour and tourist faves!
Rock pools reflecting stalactites
And icicle rocks from the floor, stalagmites.
Narrow passages and lofty chambers,
A home for Ice Age family members.

The town of Glastonbury, shrouded in mystery,
Legend and myth colour its history.
Supposedly, royalty were buried here,
King Arthur and his Queen Guinevere.
Roger and the twins enjoy views galore,
The imposing hill that is Glastonbury Tor.
And in a farmer's field near here,
The Glastonbury music festival, each year.

The legend of King Arthur abounds,
Here and the neighbouring counties around.
Near Yeovil, perched on a desolate hill,
Protected by ditches and forests, tranquil;
Was Cadbury Castle with its huge plot,
His secret palace and home, Camelot?

Over Taunton, then the Quantock Hills,
Which brush the coast where the sea overspills.
The valleys, home of the Exmoor pony
That roam free around cottages, stony.
Wild red deer in woodland, graze;
The beauty of Exmoor, all three are amazed.

For many, the most beautiful county is Devon
With sea north and south, a holiday heaven.
Thatched cottages with old wooden beams,
Lawns edged with roses, the garden of dreams.

Gliding along the North Devon coast,
Places that walkers and surfers love most,
The rugged coastline, the big rolling waves,
The cliff top walks that nature paves.
Close to the Naval shipyard, Appledore
Where two rivers meet, the Torridge and Taw.
Will Jenny or Lenny be the first spotter
To see these rivers of *Tarka the Otter*?
Henry Williamson wrote these tales
And now people walk the 'Tarka Trail'.
Lynmouth to Ilfracombe and views most handsome;
Bideford, Great Torrington and south to Okehampton.

Map of Devon and Cornwall

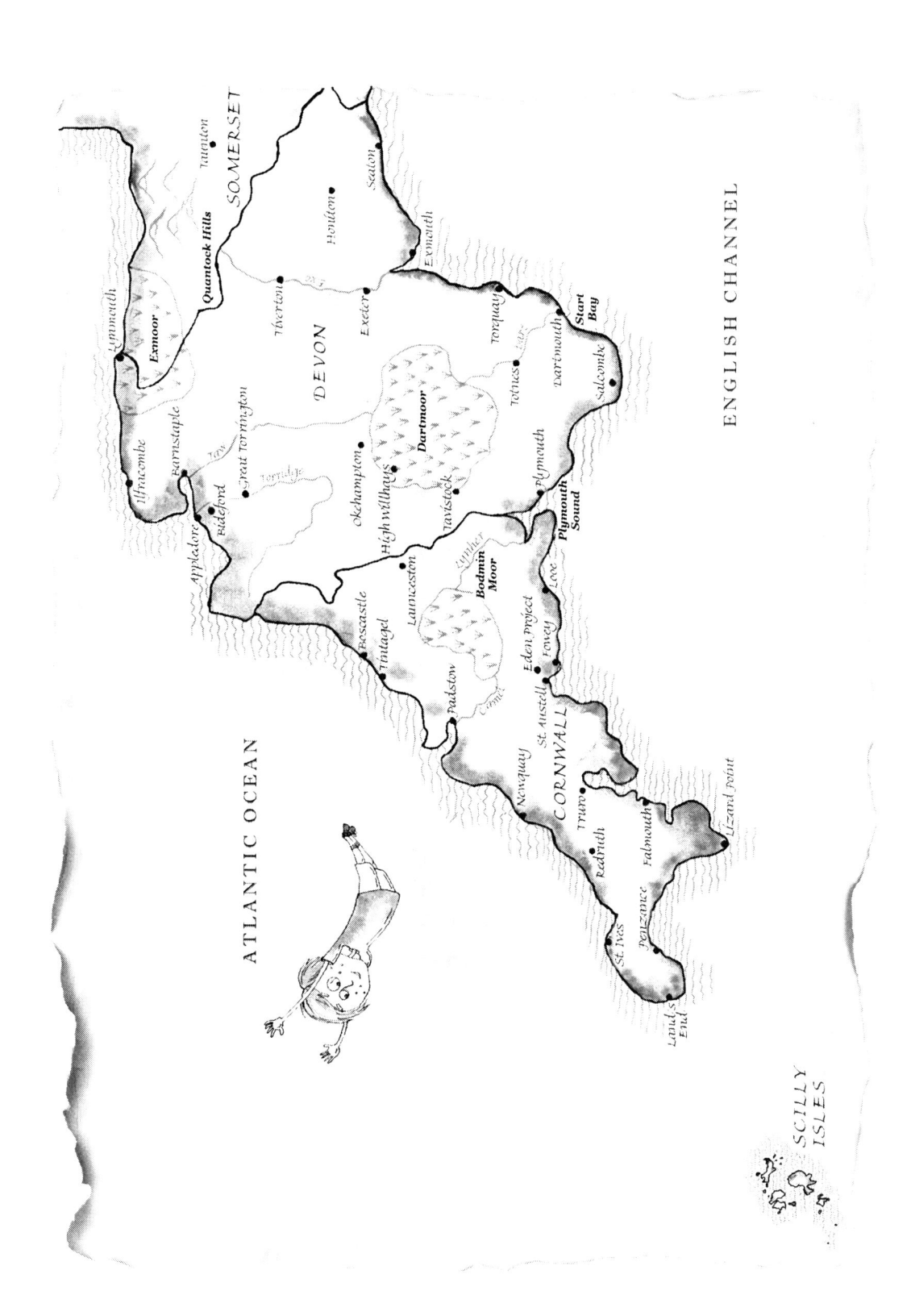

SOMERSET
- Taunton
- Quantock Hills
- Exmoor
- Lynmouth
- Tiverton
- Honiton
- Exeter
- Exmouth
- Seaton

DEVON
- Ilfracombe
- Barnstaple
- Appledore
- Bideford
- Great Torrington
- Taw
- Torridge
- Okehampton
- High Willhays
- Dartmoor
- Tavistock
- Torquay
- Totnes
- Dart
- Dartmouth
- Start Bay
- Salcombe
- Plymouth
- Plymouth Sound

CORNWALL
- Boscastle
- Tintagel
- Launceston
- Bodmin Moor
- Tamar
- Lynher
- Looe
- Padstow
- Camel
- Eden Project
- Fowey
- St Austell
- Newquay
- Truro
- Redruth
- Falmouth
- Lizard Point
- Penzance
- St Ives
- Land's End

SCILLY ISLES

ATLANTIC OCEAN

ENGLISH CHANNEL

Getting to Know Kernow

Although a county on English land;
Cornwall, through history has made a stand.
A Celtic state, centuries ago;
It was called by its Cornish name, Kernow.
The county prospered in early times
Largely, through the copper and tin mines.

Defeat to the Saxons changed Cornwall's fate
In 926 – and up to Henry VIII,
Who killed many of the Catholic people;
He pulled down their churches and their steeples.

Today the locals think it's so perfect,
They'd rather continue to speak their own dialect.
They're rightly proud of their county's history.
Here, Roger tells of King Arthur's mystery.

'Arthur was born in the town of Tintagel;
His Queen was Guinevere, beautiful yet fragile.
She was also loved by the knight, Sir Lancelot;
You already know their castle was Camelot.
Merlin the magician's advice kept him stable;
He fought alongside the "knights of the round table".
His sword, Excalibur, was thrown into a lake
Then caught by a female hand, for Arthur's sake.

For it was said, this gave him life;
Where was this lake? Rumour was rife.
On Bodmin Moor at Dozmary Pool?
Or down near Lizard Point, Loe Pool?'

Cornwall's north coast has beautiful places
With wooded valleys and rocky faces.
Seaside towns that have no match;
Fishing boats groan with the weight of the catch.
Boscastle, Padstow and down to Newquay;
Again, a place where the surfers will be.

Long sandy beaches to the town of St Ives
And friendly faces where tourism thrives.
To Land's End, England's most westerly point;
The most southerly is across at Lizard Point.

Around thirty miles out to sea,
The three fly off to the Isles of Scilly.
Renowned for colourful flowers and fruit,
The warmer climate here does suit.
However, in fog, sea captains must check
Every detail… or become a shipwreck!

Over the turquoise waters they dance
Back to the mainland, the port of Penzance.
Then round the Lizard Peninsula they go,
Red and black cliffs and a windswept plateau.
The Helford River with its secretive creeks
And coves, ideal for pirates and sneaks.

On to St Austell, then they soon pass
The Eden Project in a huge house of glass.
Tropical weather within these curved walls
For exotic plants, palm trees and waterfalls!
The three fly low, they skim the waves
Like seagulls swooping down on their prey.
From Fowey to Looe they hug the shore,
Then over the Tamar – Cornwall no more.

A Little Slice of Devon

Jenny's the first to land on the ground
Back into Devon by Plymouth Sound.
Roger offers them something tasty,
A souvenir of Cornwall, a Cornish pasty!
The twins tuck in to the pastry treat
With potatoes, swede and seasoned meat.
Then scones and jam – Devonshire Cream Teas,
While Roger has many more stories to please.

'Sir Francis Drake left England behind
To sail round the world on the *Golden Hind*.
In 1577, he left
Plymouth Sound for Africa, West.
Across the Atlantic, down to Brazil,
Then round the Magellan Strait, a thrill.
Back up the west of South America,
Past Chile, Mexico and North America.
Then the Pacific, one long great motion
To Indonesia, then the Indian Ocean.
South of India and Africa's East Coast,
A journey so draining and tiring, most.
But just when he thought he may not cope,
The bottom of Africa and the Cape of Good Hope!
Up passed Namibia, Angola, Cameroon,
Sir Francis was feeling over the moon!

The islands Cape Verde, the Canaries and Spain,
Portugal, France and then home again!'

'Sir Francis was England's first round the world.
But lately it was done, alone, by a girl.
Ellen MacArthur, round all the world's bays;
An achievement so amazing, in seventy-one days!'

'Plymouth is a large Royal Navy base;
For many discoveries, the starting place.
Captain Cook left here for Australia
While Scott set sail for the South Pole – Antarctica!'

'Sir Francis Drake was at it again,
In 1588, with all his men.
While playing bowls he was trying harder
Than in battle with the Spanish Armada!
He tested the wind direction with his finger,
So on the green, he decided to linger.
"There's a strong headwind, so we can wait
And finish this game and still not be late."
He won at bowls, his opponents were vanquished,
Now to the port to defeat the Spanish.'

'Sir Walter Raleigh was another great seaman;
He sailed, like Drake, in times Elizabethan.
From the Americas, he brought back tobacco
And many say Raleigh introduced the potato.
He too, for his Queen Elizabeth was loyal;
He fought the Armada in his ship, the *Ark Royal*.

A hero, he put down the Irish Rebellion
But later spent time in prison, a villain.
King James I wanted peace with Spain
But Raleigh attacked them again and again!
He stole from the Spanish, this news the King dreaded
So he jailed Raleigh, then had him beheaded!'

Away from Plymouth, over Dartmoor they pass
Hills and bogs and flat heathery grass.
Wooded gorges and waterfalls;
A mysterious blanket of mist enthrals.
High Willhays is the highest peak –
'The Roof of Devon' at over 2,000 feet.

Dartmouth sits on the River Dart
Where many of the Navy made a start.
The sailors studied and gained lots of knowledge
At the Royal Britannia Naval College.
A famous author and queen of mystery
Who lived nearby was Agatha Christie.

Just south of here down at Start Bay,
In World War II, training for D-Day;
The army practised their sea to beach landings
For the brave and vital Normandy landings
Where many young men died on the shore;
But it meant the allies would win the war…

Jurassic Lark

Dorset is Thomas Hardy country;
A designated area of outstanding beauty.
This famous author wrote many of his books
Set amongst Dorset's babbling brooks.
There's Blackmoor Vale and Cranborne Chase;
Country life at a slower pace.
However, Roger, ahead and above
Has interesting stories that Lenny will love.

'The Jurassic coast from Exmouth to Poole;
Millions of years of history, so cool.
Take your bucket and spade to the sand,
On beaches, you can find fossils by hand!
All close by and within easy reach,
The ten-mile strip at Chesil Beach.
Further east near Lulworth Cove;
Discovered – a recent treasure trove.
Dinosaur footprints were found near here,
Just recently, in the last ten years!'

'Outside Dorchester, a few miles from sea
At Maiden Castle, a gruesome discovery.
Thirty-eight skeletons under the stones
With fragments of Roman weapons in their bones!'

'Up on a hill, a carving so rude
At Cerne Abbas, a giant man, nude!
His body is 180 feet long;
He's holding a club that makes him look strong.

Jenny and Lenny just giggle away
As smiling Roger leads the way.
'The holiday towns of Bournemouth and Poole;
In summer, the beaches and restaurants are full.
In 1907, round and about,
Baden Powell founded the Scouts.
He taught young boys to try much harder
At Brownsea Island in Poole Harbour.'

'In 1708, there were two little ships
From Poole, that sailed on adventurous trips.
On this occasion, a storm blew them south
Past bay and cove and harbour mouth.
They drifted off course, confusion on deck;
They came to an island and a man shipwrecked.
This stranded man, Alexander Selkirk,
His plight inspired a great piece of work:
His story was told to Daniel Defoe
Who then wrote a book – *Robinson Crusoe*!'

The stunning New Forest was a royal hunting ground
With beautiful scenery all around.
There are oaks and redwoods and conifer trees
And open heath for wild roaming ponies.

'Buried here in this sacred soil
Is the writer, Sir Arthur Conan Doyle.
He created the detective, Sherlock Holmes,
Who picked through crimes with a fine tooth comb.
And buried in Lyndhurst, right in the middle
Is a lady by the name of Alice Liddell.
Well, actually her tombstone, would you believe
Is marked with the name, Mrs Reginald Hargreaves!
For Lewis Carroll, this Alice did stand
As the inspiration for *Alice in Wonderland*.'

'In 1100, that was the year,
A king was killed while hunting for deer.
William Rufus, in broad daylight
Was shot with an arrow by a Norman knight.
Accident or murder or was he just cursed?
Some said his brother, Henry I
Ordered his murder so that would bring
Henry the crown and the title of King!
The spot where William fell with a groan
Is marked with a monument – Rufus Stone.'

Between the rivers, Itchen and Test;
The port of Southampton, one of England's best.
Cruise liners travel to the old world and new,
And birthed here the world renowned QE2.
The luxury liner with butlers and staff;
They don't do anything here by half!

'In 1912, RMS *Titanic*
Sailed west across the icy Atlantic.
It hit an iceberg late at night;
Hours later, it was out of sight.
It broke in half, two mighty chunks
That slipped beneath the waves and sunk.
Nearly 1,500 died
But thankfully, around 700 survived…'

'When World War II came down to the wire,
The British were thankful for the *Spitfire*.
A Southampton man designed this plane
And R J Mitchell was his name.'

'In the 9th century, King Alfred the Great,
The only 'great' of all monarchs to date;
Inherited a kingdom where Vikings camped;
So he knew this kingdom must be revamped.
The city of Winchester was his base,
He united the Saxons to defend this place.
He showed the Vikings what a King he could be
Through battles, discussions and peace treaties.
Alfred was fair, he created new laws;
He built defences for any new wars.
He translated books so his people could learn;
With education, his people could earn.
Alfred controlled his kingdom's fate,
He was honest, clever, brave and "great".'

'Near Winchester, I can reveal
Was born Ethel Rhoda McNeile.
An English heroine, it's certainly true,
For her deed of 1922.
A ship, the *Egypt*, was sinking fast;
A lifeboat seat, she had the last.
But then she heard a voice of another,
"My poor little children will have no mother!"
So Ethel gave away her place,
An amazing member of the human race!
The *Egypt* sank off the coast of France,
Ethel stayed onboard with no chance…'

A major port by the South Downs
Is Portsmouth, the biggest of Navy towns.
'Here, there are 17,000 staff
And fifty ships, that's more than half
Of all the Royal Navy's fleet,
A fighting force that's hard to beat.
For queen and country, immensely loyal.
The *Illustrious*, *Invincible* and *Ark Royal*,
Three aircraft carriers, kings of the sea lanes
With fighter jets and reconnaissance planes.
All of the Navy's destroyers are here,
With frigates and other ships – to fear!'

'One of the world's best fighting forces,
The elite, who train on land and sea courses,
The Royal Marines – Naval infantry;
Among the best soldiers in the country.

And when they are trained and on their way,
They can wear, with pride, the Green Beret.
They are Commandos who go anywhere
And fight the battles others not dare.
On icy mountain, in tropical jungle
Or scorching desert, they're ready to rumble!'

Over the Solent, the Isle of Wight,
Dinosaur skeletons were found, that's right!
On the east coast, by Sandown and Shanklin,
Jenny and Lenny begin their searching!
While they are elbow deep in sand
They beckon Roger to give them a hand.
'There's no sign of dinosaur bones today,
Let's clean ourselves up and be on our way.
To Carisbrooke Castle, an institution,
Which held Charles II – before execution!
And Queen Victoria lived in East Cowes
With her husband, Prince Albert, at Osborne House.
Then every August, sailors compete,
Racing their yachts during Cowes Week.
Since the 1820s, a prestigious event,
Champagne for the winning ladies and gents!'

ENGLISH CHANNEL

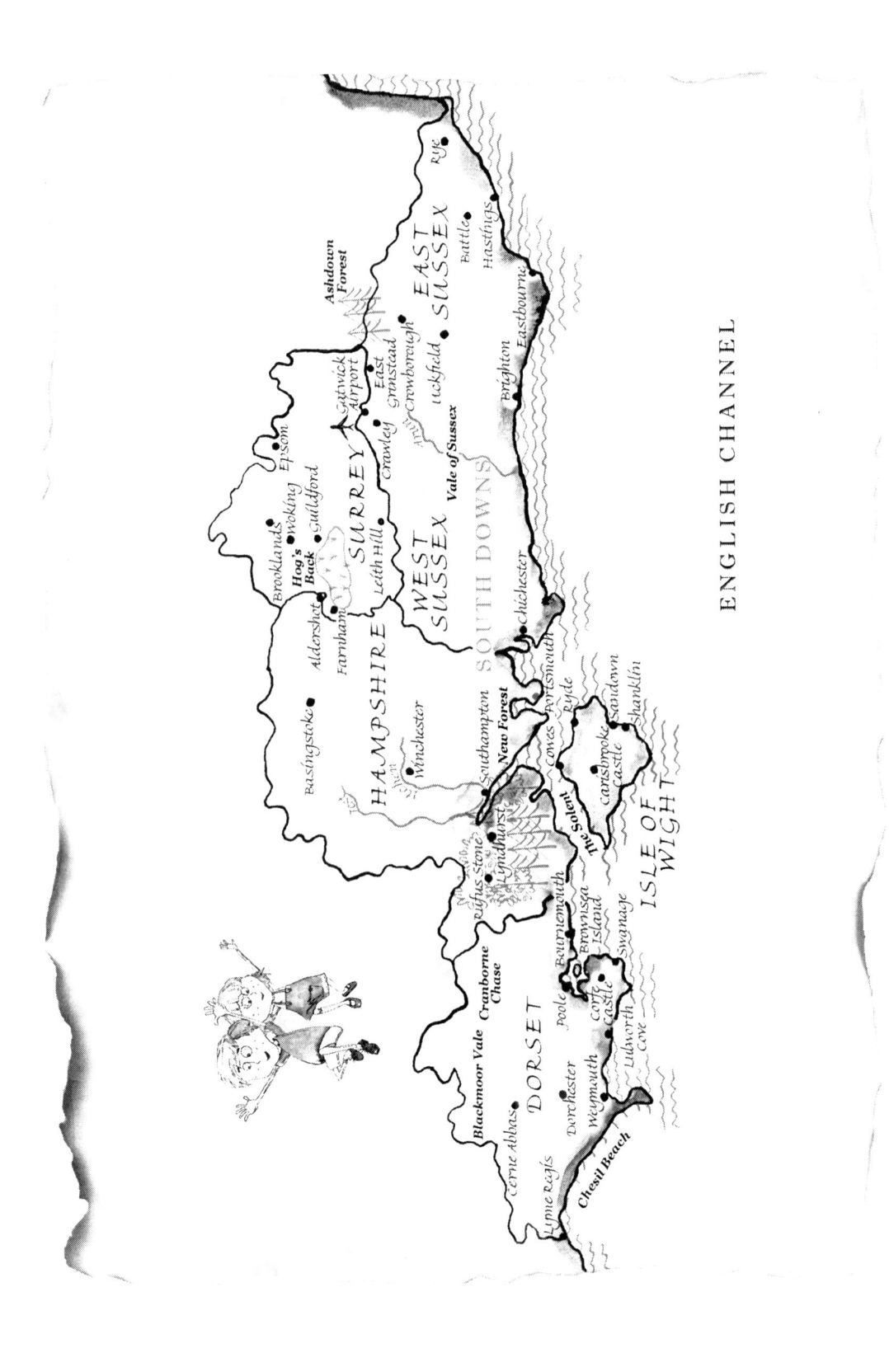

The Battle of Hastings and Other Things

Over the Channel, their flight is quite short;
Their destination, a famous resort.
And here's something they don't often teach,
At Brighton was England's first nudist beach!
An extravagant building, it's one in a million,
A grand Indian palace? No, the Brighton Pavilion!

As Jenny and Lenny look on in awe,
Roger begins to tell them more.
'At the Grand Hotel, 1984,
An IRA bomb ripped through the floors.
An act so terrible, scary and sinister,
To kill Margaret Thatcher, England's Prime Minister!
Although she and her Cabinet survived,
Thirty were injured and five people died…'

'In Hastings, 1923,
A clever man invented TV.
This was the year a programme first aired,
So say "thank goodness for John Logie Baird!"'

'Divided kingdoms with many conflicts,
Was England before 1066.
There were many battles, Saxons and Vikings;
Then the Normans and the Battle of Hastings.'

'The Saxon king, Edward the Confessor
Had died but managed to name a successor;
The Earl of Wessex became Harold II.
But from all sides, trouble beckoned!
The King of Norway, Harold Hardrada
Made the Saxons' task a lot harder.
However, Harold II won,
He saw off the Vikings, so that was done.
Of 240 ships that arrived,
Just twenty-four Viking ships survived!
The battle weary had a victory to toast
But then a long march to the south coast.
One of the most important things
In English history – the Battle of Hastings…'

'Waiting was William with the Normans from France;
A Saxon victory? A fifty-fifty chance.
Saxon foot soldiers fought with force
And battled Normans who attacked on horse.
For hours the fighting was a stalemate,
Then the Saxons made a fatal mistake.
The Normans pretended to make a retreat;
The Saxons charged and their line was breached.
Normans fired arrows into the sky;
One came down – hit Harold in the eye!
The Normans had won after Saxon error;
Their leader became King William the Conqueror.'

Roger had finished so away Lenny peeled;
Leading the way from Battle to Uckfield.
Heading north, visibility good;
To Ashdown Forest or 'Hundred Acre Wood'.
Lenny said, 'There are stories of these wooded hills,
For in Hartfield nearby, lived A A Milne;
Who wrote nice tales for me and you –
The wonderful adventures of Winnie-the-Pooh!'

Jenny smiled, again Roger was thrilled.
He led them to Dorking and Leith Hill –
South East England's highest place;
Then over the Hog's Back, they had a race.
This chalk ridge that heads out west
Near Farnham and Aldershot where they'd rest.

Roger was last to land on the ground,
'This is Aldershot, proud army town.
A soldier cannot question why,
Even though he may possibly die.
Orders are given that he must follow
No matter how hard they are to swallow.
For this is their life, a soldier's lot;
Brave soldiers from bases like Aldershot.
They defend the country and its shores;
They bravely fought and won two world wars.
They kept the Falklands from Argentina,
And two Gulf wars, now times are much meaner.'

The three take off and now they're approaching,
Just above Guildford, the town of Woking.
The Shah Jehan Mosque, for Muslims a shrine;
The oldest in England, since 1889.

Like Ascot and Aintree and other places,
Epsom is also famous for horse races.
This is where the Derby is run
With rosettes and trophies for those who have won.

Like Brands Hatch, Silverstone and other places,
Brooklands was famous for motor car races.
The first British Grand Prix, 1926,
Began a tradition, drivers got their kicks!
Then during the war were built army planes;
A home for the *Wellington* and *Hurricane*.

Around Greater London, venues of all sorts
With proud traditions and homes to all sports.
'There's Wimbledon,' said Jenny, 'And Centre Court,
Where many great tennis finals are fought.
Fred Perry of England, with shots and tricks;
He won Wimbledon, 1936.
Angela Mortimer had so much fun
When she became champion in 1961.
And another English rose so fine
Was Ann Jones, champion in 1969.
Tim Henman has tried and come very close;
He has been the one the crowd support most.

But the best result in the last thirty years,
A champion who gained the most English cheers;
She put all others in the shade
In 1977 – Virginia Wade!'

'There's Twickenham,' Lenny pipes up,
'Where England have won many a rugby cup.
They also beat Australia in Sydney
To win the World Cup in 2003!
And Wembley Stadium is over there
The home of football, to say is fair.
In FA Cup Finals, their fans are delighted,
The most FA Cups for Manchester United.
Arsenal, Tottenham and Liverpool, you'll find,
With Aston Villa, are not far behind.
However, the best of all, the pick,
England won the World Cup in 1966.
They beat West Germany with a sharp burst,
One goal from Peters and three from Geoff Hurst!'

Enfield
Barnet
Stanmore
Finchley
Chingford
Harrow School
Hendon RAF Museum
Hampstead Heath
Piccadilly Circus
Ilford
Wembley Stadium
Leicester Square
Covent Garden
Lord's Cricket Ground
The Strand
Fleet Street
Barking
Hackney
Dagenham
Ealing
Baker Street
West End
City
Tower of London
Hayes
Notting Hill
Hyde Park
Thames
Woolwich
London Eye
Westminster
Lambeth
Greenwich
Heathrow Airport
Wandsworth
Twickenham
Eltham
Richmond Park
Lewisham
Dulwich
Wimbledon
Hampton Court Palace
GREATER LONDON
Bromley
Croydon

London Calling

The skies are busy so flying is slow
Near one of the world's busiest airports – Heathrow.
Roger began, 'You know all about the jumbo jet
But the plane the British will never forget;
With triangular wings and a rather large nose
And record for speeds, boy, how it goes!
Now not in service, time no longer affords
The majestic fleet of Britain's *Concorde*.'

'Those German aircraft were very naughty
In the Battle of Britain, 1940.
Headquarters in Stanmore at Bentley Prior
Ordered the RAF to return fire.
These brave young pilots won the day;
They shot down some, while others flew away.
They saved us all, the entire country;
We must be grateful, all and sundry.
Over in Hendon, take time to see them,
The planes and stories at the RAF Museum.
Sir Winston Churchill had this view,
"Never, had so many, owed so much, to so few".'

Seven former pupils of Harrow School,
Went on to become prime ministers who'd rule.
Churchill was one and among others too
Was India's first, Pandit Nehru.

Flying in over and past Hampstead Heath,
Lenny looks down on the site beneath.
'Here is Lord's, the home of cricket,
It's very hard to get hold of a ticket!
England has won many fantastic clashes,
The best of all, the 2005 Ashes!'

Jenny points out Baker Street,
'Where Dr Watson and Sherlock Holmes meet!
There's Madame Tussaud's famous waxworks,
Where any type of celebrity lurks!'

Then Jenny suddenly banks to the right;
The other two follow, she's still just in sight.
Jenny slows down at Notting Hill;
She hears the beating of drums made of steel.
'That's the Caribbean sound, OK!
I think I can also hear some reggae.
Stalls with Jamaican and West Indian food
And everyone here's in a party mood.
Vibrant costumes and dancers, so wonderful,
That's the magic of Notting Hill Carnival!'

To Kensington Gardens and into Hyde Park,
Around the Serpentine, the three of them lark.
They land for a moment on top of a bandstand,
Then off to the statue of Peter Pan.
To Speakers' Corner, what's that all about?
A man on a box then begins to shout,

'The end is nigh, the end is nigh!'
Roger tuts then lets out a sigh.
'Come on you two, let's go out that end
And head across town to see Big Ben.'

The 320-foot high clock tower,
Its bells ring out over London each hour.
The Houses of Parliament, debates and talks;
Almost blown up by that man, Guy Fawkes!
To Westminster Abbey, where monarchs are crowned;
For centuries, before the Normans were around.
Then over the Thames for another view,
St Thomas' Hospital, the station, Waterloo.
The world's biggest observation wheel – high,
With views all around, the London Eye.
Then back over Westminster Bridge they glide;
The Prime Minister's house on the other side,
10 Downing Street with its black front door,
Near Horse Guards Parade, just off Whitehall.
To King Charles Street where history looms,
In World War II, the Cabinet War Rooms.
Here, Sir Winston Churchill stayed,
Tending to the country's affairs of the day.
He, his Cabinet and advisers would meet
In the basement under buildings and concrete.
With a shooting range, hospital, bedrooms, canteen;
Safe from the Germans, he was rarely seen.

The Union Flag of red, white and blue,
Lines the Mall, guiding them through

To the house at the end of the road – now seen,
Buckingham Palace, the home of the Queen!
Since 1837 and Queen Victoria
To today, where all three feel the euphoria.

Roger recalled, 'In the front yard,
Every morning, the Changing of the Guard.
Inspecting her troops, the Queen's very thorough;
A weekend in June, Trooping the Colour.
Many monarchs, before Buckingham Palace,
Lived and reigned at Hampton Court Palace.'
'Oh yes,' said Lenny, 'it's not far away,
Jenny and I were in the maze all day!'

Over Green Park, they're excited to bits;
To Piccadilly Circus, bright lights and glitz!
Shoppers on Regent and Oxford Streets;
Restaurants, fast food, all types of eats.
Theatres with plays, dance and song;
Tourists and Londoners, a bustling throng.
In Leicester Square, graces and airs,
The special red carpet for film premieres.
Chinatown is well worth a glance;
Especially a Chinese New Year dragon dance!
Covent Garden, with roast chestnut vendors;
The Royal Opera House with sopranos and tenors.
A mime artist performs in the street,
While other dancers jive to the beat.

'Soon,' said Roger, 'We'll go and eat.
But – around the corner in Bow Street
Henry Fielding had an idea,
In 1750, that was the year.
He set up the Bow Street Runners, that time,
Good honest men who tried to stop crime.
Then in 1830, to keep the peace,
Sir Robert Peel founded the Police.
These boys in blue stopped illegal hobbies,
After Sir Robert, they're still nicknamed 'bobbies'.
But now as promised, we'll go and have dinner,
I know a great place, it's a real winner.'

The hungry trio as fast as was able
Had flown and were now seated at a table!
'Wow!' exclaimed Lenny, 'They have cottage pie,
And there are other dishes that have caught my eye.
Roast beef and Yorkshire pudding with gravy,
Steak and kidney pie – just maybe.
There's cod and haddock and Dover sole,
Mashed potatoes with toad-in-the-hole.
That's plump sausages in pancake batter,
That's what I'll have, I'll have the latter.'
'Roast chicken,' Jenny asserts,
'Then we must have a number of desserts!
Apple crumble, then sherry trifle;
Lemon meringue pie – that's quite an eyeful!
Jam roly-poly and spotted dick,
Treacle sponge with custard, thick.

Roger, please, can we have this lot,
And wash it down with dandelion and burdock?'

Roger obliges these gluttonous twins;
One smile from Jenny – she always wins!
As they all gorge, Roger starts a tale:
'A very famous nurse, Florence Nightingale.
In hospital or even army camp,
She was known as "the lady with the lamp".
She tended the sick; she cared for them well;
The Crimean War, a living hell.
In 1854, in Turkey,
She made each soldier's life less murky.
She wrote letters home to their families,
She did their banking, she sent home moneys.
She saved many lives from being lost,
She was awarded the Order of the British Red Cross.'

'The Duke of Wellington was a hero too;
He won the Battle of Waterloo.
Napoleon tried to take his chance
To take over Europe and claim it for France.
However, in Belgium, 1815,
The British and Allies were mightily keen.
They held firm, they stayed in the trench;
There was confusion among the French.
Their forces depleted, wounded and tender;
This forced Napoleon to surrender.'

London's Burning

On the restaurant walls, some majestic art;
For Roger, another topic to start.
'England has many artists of note,
Three from history who get my vote:
Stunning both, Constable and Gainsborough,
However, my favourite of all was Turner.
He would study the weather for days;
Thunderous skies with colours to amaze.
Bolts of lightning out of the blue;
He always managed to capture the view.
So detailed, he never did things by half;
His paintings, as real as a photograph!'

'Over in Greenwich, a special line,
Some may say the beginning of time!
The world is cut in two right here,
The western and eastern hemispheres.
In any country, the time it will be
Is linked to Greenwich Mean Time – GMT.'

The greatest English author was Charles Dickens;
His vivid story telling, the plot always thickens.
Larger than life characters like Oliver Twist
And Scrooge from *A Christmas Carol* can't be missed.
A Tale of Two Cities and *Great Expectations*
Today, still thrill many of the world's nations.

A knocked over glass, a drink has been spilled,
Time for Roger to pay the bill!
The three get up from the dining table
With big full tummies, to fly they're unable!
'Come on you two, take my hand,'
Roger decided, 'We'll walk down the Strand.
We'll go for a stroll, we'll use our feet,
We'll see the newspaper houses on Fleet Street.
Then the Old Bailey, famous law courts,
They try bad criminals, all nasty sorts.
A century ago, on this spot
Was Newgate Prison where they were left to rot!
On to St Paul's Cathedral, then;
Designed by the architect, Sir Christopher Wren.
The Great Fire of London, 1666,
Had given Sir Christopher the chance to fix
The burned down cathedral, which he did with glee;
Now home to weddings and any Royal Jubilee.'

'The Great Fire started in Pudding Lane
At the Royal bakery with a timber frame.
The wooden houses were all alight,
The fire raged for four days and four nights.
Londoners fled, they were all afraid;
There was no such thing as a fire brigade!
Amazingly, only five people died,
But 13,000 houses were fried.
Eighty-seven churches burnt down,
200,000 were left homeless in town…'

The Bank of England is now within range;
Here is the City and the Stock Exchange.
But the three of them stay close to the river;
A cool breeze gives them a shiver.
Past London Bridge and sightseeing charms;
To Tower Bridge with its two moving arms!
Each arm weighs 1,000 tonnes;
They rise once a day when a big ship comes.

On the bridge the three take a walk,
Then Roger points and begins to talk.
'There is the Tower of London so fine;
A place of execution for crime.
Also a fortress, a prison with rules
And home to the world famous Crown Jewels!'

Suddenly, Roger is pushed to the ground,
Three nasty men tell him, 'Stay down!
You little kiddies, you'll go to the Tower
For this will be your very last hour!
You've heard of the princes, you must be aware
Of how they went missing, murdered up there!'

Roger tried to get up on his feet
But two of the men held him down on the street.
'Run away you two, I'll be all right,
I'll show these evil men I can fight!'
Jenny and Lenny with tears in their eyes
Flapped their arms but neither could fly!

Still weighed down with trifle and crumble,
Jenny goes first but takes a stumble.
Lenny grabs her arm and they run
While Roger kicks one of the men up the bum!

He grapples and wrestles with two on the floor,
However, the third gives chase and is sure
That he can capture these innocent twins,
With blackened teeth he laughs and grins.

'Jenny,' said Lenny, 'It's clear we can't fly.
We'll hide somewhere and he'll pass on by.
Let's move fast, I have an idea,
We'll do what the king did in yesteryear.'
Away from the bridge and down a side road,
As fast as they can with a tummy full load!
Lenny grabs Jenny by the hand,
The time has come to make their stand.
'This is it Jenny, we'll head for that oak
And climb up and hide from this wicked bloke.
Just like King Charles II had done;
He hid from the Roundheads in 1651.'

Jenny and Lenny were out of sight
They picked out the oak tree just to their right.
Lenny clasped his hands like a cup
And hauled his sister up and up.
When she was safe on a branch quite high,
He followed her quick and looked up to the sky.

He joined his hands and said a prayer
That they'd be safe from this nightmare.
Jenny looked down and saw the man!
However he passed, and ran and ran
Until he was no longer in sight.
Thanks to history, Lenny was right!

The alarm clock rings, there are two sleepy heads.
And soon they will have to get out of their beds.
Jenny opens her eyes to see
That they are not stuck up in a tree!
'Oh Lenny, Lenny, it was all a dream!
So there were no nasty men, so mean.'

'Come on,' cried Mum, 'I'm not going to beg.
Come down and eat your bacon and eggs.'
The two come down and the telephone rings,
It turns out the call is for either of the twins.
'I am your Mother but I feel like a lodger,
Here, take the phone, it's your new friend, Roger!'

SCOTLAND
WALES
Newcastle-upon-Tyne
Sunderland
Carlisle
Middlesbrough
Scarborough
Kendal
York
Leeds
Blackpool
Manchester
Grimsby
Liverpool
Sheffield
Chester
Lincoln
Stoke-on-Trent
Nottingham
Derby
Grantham
Leicester
King's Lynn
Norwich
Shrewsbury
Birmingham
Coventry
Worcester
Northampton
Bedford
Cambridge
Ipswich
Hereford
Colchester
Gloucester
Oxford
St Albans
Southend-on-Sea
London
Bristol
Windsor
Guildford
Canterbury
Bath
Salisbury
Dover
Taunton
Southampton
Hastings
Brighton
Poole
Exeter
ISLE OF WIGHT
Plymouth
Newquay
Land's End
SCILLY ISLES

About the Author

K M G Woodbury was born in London but has lived in a number of different countries and has a passion for the many wonderful cultures that enrich the world.

After working on an advertising campaign for a children's swimming aid, he was inspired to try and do more to help children learn. With this book on England, the first in the series, he wishes to share with children that the world is truly a magical place.

Printed in the United Kingdom
by Lightning Source UK Ltd.
128000UK00002B/1-4/P